SIGNS

For

Lilian Mary Wicker
1929 - 1996

SIGNS

George Wicker

Published 2007 by arima publishing

www.arimapublishing.com

ISBN 978-1-84549-178-9

© George Wicker 2007

All rights reserved

This book is copyright. Subject to statutory exception and to provisions of relevant collective licensing agreements, no part of this publication may be reproduced, stored in a retrieval system, or transmitted in any form or by any means, without the prior written permission of the author.

Printed and bound in the United Kingdom

Typeset in Palatino Linotype

This book is sold subject to the conditions that it shall not, by way of trade or otherwise, be lent, re-sold, hired out, or otherwise circulated without the publisher's prior consent in any form of binding or cover other than that in which it is published and without a similar condition including this condition being imposed on the subsequent purchaser.

Swirl is an imprint of arima publishing

arima publishing
ASK House, Northgate Avenue
Bury St Edmunds, Suffolk IP32 6BB
t: (+44) 01284 700321

www.arimapublishing.com

Acknowledgements

Some of these poems were first published in Breathe, Inverse, Pulsar and The Black Rose magazines

Dead Flowers, Horizon, The Stream, Speckled Universe and Fate first appeared in Jade, (Inverse Press 1997)

Contents

That First Man	1
Pharaoh	2
Camera Lucida	3
Certain Artists	4
Technology	6
Uncovering	8
Poets	9
Poetry	10
Signs	12
Dunwich	13
War	15
Losing It	17
We Were Free	18
To a Young Girl	19
Before You	20
Haunted House	21
I Have Loved	22
Seeing You	23
The Stream	24
Feline	25
Crocodiles	27
Nature	28
Voices	29
When the Sickness Descends	31
Anticipation	33

Dead Flowers	34
Reunion	36
Solid Rock	37
Today	38
It Is Wrong	40
The Space Between	41
Stars	43
Speckled Universe	44
Night	46
Key of Dawn	47
A Puzzle	49
Time	51
An Audience	53
The Way	54
River	56
The Path	57
Fate	58

That First Man

What made that first man
pick up his stone and send
scratches sprawling
in multiplying efficiency

of purpose over the white bone?
Torn from a carcase,
scrawled on at leisure,
with that action came

hooting and laughing
as his slow brain resided in
the graven image. What
came to him there,

when for the first time,
he looked at his art, seeing
only inadequate show
of his own poor frame?

He was fixed in that first wonder,
no longer stooping,
as the pleasurable mind-grow
began in pain.

Pharaoh

It is not about how
a comet finds its way to a sun,
or a word to a page, a greeting across
lines of electromagnetic communication.
We designed it like this,
lived in it for a while, spoke
words of courage about its maker,
dreamed we could fashion something similar.

These actions came to haunt me:
alone, in a disgraced cell
I dictate patterns to bad taste
then call it rubbish and walk away.
Victim of fashion, superfluous
style, adjunct to bitter divorce, battle
over whose painting, what bed linen.

Sign the paper and seal the sarcophagus,
better have walked the planet
although I can't find them,
having renewed the effort
as a pharaoh once spied on the heavens
to see the sun of the same name.

Camera Lucida

You know it was easy
the way he demonstrated it.
That prism—so fine!
The image came senseless
and swam into a split vision;
subject above, shot of the hand
below, as it traced out
a masterpiece.

Camera lucida, to show us where
we have been, and why
things didn't work out
so well. The split image
that carved up life; on the one side
what we imagined,
and on the other
reality.

Certain Artists

I do not know the horizon
but I look for it anyway;
that flat piece of land
tacked on the edge of a desert
or hidden behind trees:
the oasis of the painters.
Look for it I say, scouring the endless
panorama of days
until the summer ends,
the sky fizzles out,
the blue comes down like a balloon
and it all simply flaps away.

What lies beyond the horizon
that we will never reach, what lies
behind it I say, trying to tether
the useless plastic flaps of society
into place, so I continue to order
food, sofas, toys for the child?
I'll tell you what lies behind
if I ever reach it
through indomitable faith, bad luck
or even worse judgement.

The world is flat, the horizon thin;
certain artists tempt me to say
it is within our grasp.
Certain artists
could be wrong, myself included.

Technology

The message I got
when I finally tuned in
was that the planet was dead.
I moved on, through wavelengths

long abandoned. Next I heard
in a whirl of static, that she had left me!
I put the listener right
on that score. Megahertz later,

a voice was singing a song
so pure, unwavering, like a lark's lament
way above scorched fields,
like all the sisters of hell

finally calmed down, singing
the simplicity of themselves
while heaven rained around them
in its earthly guise.

So, the ethereal music
took me out of myself, out of
the radio, which after all
is simply something I made

from the mechanism of life,
out of the ghosts and graves of technology;
where this song took me
was some place more, sincere.

Uncovering

I followed the pattern
like the book said, only
it wasn't a book
but something in my head.

I traced an outline
the book told me was real
only, my head wasn't real,
just what was inside it.

So I separated spirit from the flesh
and rose, like a book from its cover,
except that it was only words.
The good thing was; it was only words.

So the spirit rose above
as the body stayed below,
counting the hours
in useless harmony of days.

Poets

As we fly
tangential to things
it is only proper that poets,
versed in sorrow,
echoing the dead religions,
pierce the undiluted filth
with an even filthier cry.

Poetry

It can describe a sunset
that colour-floods a town
or rabbits on a lawn, at dawn;
a nature of eccentricities.

It can describe sorrow
love, bereavement, pain.
The simple world of images,
flesh carved in a man's name,
bring to our attention terror,
the repetition of error.

But can it describe the blank stare
of a population passing days in boredom,
of a life without observation
light, love or lover?

Can it describe the lack of meaning,
the long days passing, leaning
ever more quickly to one release—
dreaded by most—death.

Can it describe anger, frustration?
The line of poor at the rich man's elbow,
can it describe this world without colour,

without God, without feeling
there is nothing left to discover
except one's own disappearing
never to recover?

Signs

A coughing, spluttering fit.
A nervous, high laugh.
sign of spring—bird song;
sign of winter—long scarf
wrapped around the throat.
A sharp frost, a dull pain;
there are signs of life in me,
signs of death too, age
creeps up, as winter does
then leaves, as life should do
by transition, not by this sudden
snatch of death, the soul away
the body cold, the crocus old;
end of the short, short day.

Dunwich

Dunwich, where the graves
show themselves in time, half in
or half out of the cliffs
above the sea, where bones
once came alive and danced
down to the beach they say.

All comes to the base of things;
a dog picks up a bone and runs,
heedless of the scale of time,
along the shingle with its catch.
A skull rolls over with a kick—
its laughing eyes, their sockets blind
mist in meaning, mocking:

We were once men, we ran and played,
saw the strands of this great town
eroded by the waves.
Nothing that we could have saved:
as men return to God, but doubt
the efficacy of return, so all things,
their stones or bones, return to clay.

We found fossils on that beach,
stooping among the flints and pebbles:

insect wings half-held in stone
like the graveyard gripped above,
relinquishing its load;
a fragment of a prehistoric shell.

Each civilisation is founded on another,
ages of man roll under and are
buried. Nothing disturbs
the crusts of time. In pulse alone,
vibration of the ether, the solitary
tear of time, we are phantoms,
ghosts, and elements of ruin.

War

Children, join hands
it may not be
that you will fight
for your country.

Children, sing songs
gather in play
you may not be here
another day.

Children, give love
to the people around.
They need your wishes
to keep them sound.

Especially parents
who struggle to bring
meaning to the world
you live in.

Children be glad
that you are not old.
Children be sad
that you are not told

why the world of adults
circles around
painting the ground
painting the ground

with blood.

Losing It

Once, when a child, our ball spun over
a neighbour's wall. A beast like Hitler,
small and mad, as he stabbed
his ceremonial sword
air escaped, like a soul.
He's dead now so he couldn't cheat
life, and the ball
belonged anyway to the school.

We Were Free

Out of the ashes
of chaos
was born the world
and we were happy to have it.

Out of the sea
of darkness was born light
and we were happy to see
what we had been without.

Out of the muddle of mind
was born order
and we were happy to see
how much we could make from it.

We fashioned society
we created liberty
we scorned death;
we were free.

Then out of that order
came chaos, was born
the horror of indignity;
the monster of war.

To a Young Girl

Beside the path
where lovers walk
there is a world
where grief tips in,
and a broken heart
never mends in the time
it takes to say
I love you,
but in the time it takes
to forget
I love you.

Only then can you start
thinking again
believing again
loving again.

Before You

I stood before you
a man, tied to that cloth,
yet like you lost.

Because my body
let me in, to that group
most despised, loved, despised
of women, you hurt me.

Betraying your amazing skills
for wounding, each day
invisible cracks appeared
in my sanity.

I needed to protect you;
instead we flew apart,
the sinew of hope was twisted,
love forced from the heart.

So that, I left before you did,
and faced the stinging rain.
And now the bitter pain
and now the bitterest pain.

Haunted House

This house is haunted;
your presence here
invites, after these years
cynicism and doubt.

Only when emotions
are checked (so my severe
doctrine of denial runs),
can peace be obtained.

But your ghost moves
effortlessly through walls,
as at a seance
when curtains are lifted,

destroying my illusions.

I Have Loved

How else would I know
the effects of love?
How like a bell
that rings for the heart
sometimes to beckon,
at other times a death knell
that seems to stricken.

The broken note of its cracked shape
shatters the heart,
reveals itself cruel,
its sole purpose to instil
more torment and suffering
until rejection
seems the nearest thing to a solution.

Seeing You

This hopeful expression
of love, seeing you,
is in writing a poem,
an ode, to do

what no others could.
Few expressions tell that tale:
no story, however well
expounded, will sell

your image, yet I try to.
Approaching that perfection, love
survives in a way of living;
poetry, what I am giving

to worlds to spite what is.
And with what might be,
was.

The Stream

The stream has died
that watered love:
the bed is rock, the pillow, grass.
The head, reclining, mirrors
its regretful past
and leans, gently backwards.

Thus love dies;
the wound that lost love
opened, in the fold of the heart
so that raw
experience rushed in
has closed now.
Time pushes me out
once more into the world.

Feline

You're a cat all right,
don't know anything
but cat things, at the back door
squealing to come in,
looking for scraps, comfort,
the food that no one else brings you.

You're a cat all right,
collar against fleas,
face against mine, just
want some comfort, anything
this time in the morning,
early, and I'm writing.

Is it love? Or is your tongue
just searching for salt, is it love
that brings you back through the night?
Knowing that if nothing
better comes up, the hope will be
that one day, when your ninth life
has leached away, you will take
some of that affection with you.

May it wash off on me,
because I often need

the crumbs of comfort,
the warmth of a hand,
the fur of delight,
rubbing against me,
through me.

Crocodiles

An intense feeling of disgust—
crocodiles!
Silly flap-faced things,
how could they harm
how could one come to harm?
Crocodiles!
Teeth like a salmon's spine,
eye like a pebble
washed at the moonlit fringes
along the edge of a lake.

Nature

In the forest of the city
the tortured shapes one sees
are men, and not trees.

Voices

She stirs,
then all around her
they stir, their voices
betray them, as she
draws nearer.

They have always been there,
asleep or awake;
they talk to my Mother
and plan her escape.
Sing to her softly
or shout, so that she
echoes their obscenity.

We took off early, to University
and never came back.
Full-time, part-time, nothing:
job, life, mother;
she took our youth
and made it run, we
took her strength.

I couldn't give it back, she wouldn't
take it, that's how she was.
Never read a book, or poem, still

she knew what she wanted.
She leans now, a grey twig,
heavily on the old man,
unaware of what it's come to,
unaware of where she's going.

I hope to meet her still
in the next life, not as she is now
but as I remember her. With a will
stronger than seemed fair
at the time, but always
with love. I loved her,
we all loved her;
never had a chance to tell her.

When the Sickness Descends

I want to take her hand
and lead her to the park,
there to sit and quietly wonder
why all the sickness in the world
isn't distributed in equal portions.

Some suffer, I am saying, more than others.

If all this illness were gathered up,
couldn't we all just get a cold
and forget about the nasty things?
Of which dementia
is the worse; slow decay
of the brain, vitality and love
for the ones you used to cherish.

Mother,
it is not right
that you should disappear like this
into a world of your own making.

Mum,
It is hard to watch you
vanish into the workings of your mind
with not a word of sympathy,
for those left behind.

Forgive us, for not understanding
sickness, or the need it has
to destroy our families, to cleanse the mass
of spent souls.

Anticipation

If you are near me
tonight, if you hear me
tonight, let me know.

By the twitch of a curtain,
the breeze from a door
locked since the evening.

I haven't felt anything
but I so want something
to be unusual.

To look in the mirror
and see something
more than reflection.

To point at my map
and say
this wasn't always the road.

Dead Flowers

The vase was plain,
of plainest glass.
The stems were green,
of greenest grass,
until you reached the flowers.
For they were dead
and had been dead
for hours.

Not in some other sense alive?
Like the dead we bury to survive
ourselves, crying out in fear
for the death not yet here?

We burn, flowers wilt
we crackle, they bend
we wither, we stoop,
they stand, they grow,
we feel pain, they don't know
pain, unless it is in
the cycle of stony growth
that they adhere to.

Dead flowers around her
that were once alive.

She grows with them
now, while outside
they dismantle the flesh
with dry flame, and laughing
I hear her say
that one day
all memory is gone.

Afterwards
I walked on the Heath
with family. Do not tell me
she is dead, I do not know
that the death she had is where
I want to go, nor the way she went—
I want to stay
for the loneliest, longest day.

Reunion

In what form
I shall meet her again
I do not know—none can.
The secrets of death
are hidden from man.
We can only wonder
sitting on our thrones of earth
how the scene might pan out.
Cherubs everywhere? I doubt it,
angels all about, wings
beating the silver air
that composes clouds of wonder,
from which the Great
blows his faith, which becomes dream
that floats down to the Earth
to irritate the wealthy,
console the poor?

Solid Rock

So hard to chisel out
something from life
that facing rock
is the next best thing.

Some go up, grabbing
air, footholds, reaching for
the thing they are most frightened of
outside themselves.

Others go through
impenetrable thicket of stone
with fingernails
translating pain

into blood; a tunnel
thus is poured
through the black rock
lit by fear.

Today

People will wake up
on a planet with two suns,
cast off the crucifix of conscience
and drive their guns
into the city.

They will be no more aware
of us than we are of them.

They will say they are evolved
as we do too
and mow down any pedestrian
for being in their way
for they are powerful
on their planet.

Which is no bigger than an apple.
Could be anywhere; your garden,
mine. In fact
I trod on one today,
all squeaky flesh
long since fallen
on damp grass.

The suns could have been oranges,
other apples, planets
waiting to ripen.

It is Wrong

The lane is twisted, the house
lies round the other way.
It is not as I remember
and now fades, like the summer
of the year in which our mission failed.

We ride back to the planet
not knowing anything
better than nothing;
just a little teardrop
between stars.

The Space Between

In between stars,
pauses
of a conversation:
words, sentences, planets,
you will find us.

Light fails
darkness
comes, and sight
flickers outside your range
when we appear.

We are living
here; your thoughts
make us visible,
fears keep us
alive.

Danger for you, there
where space slips
and vision
loses its meaning,
we stare

back to the beginning—

then there was no space, only
a theory, only
a word, not even
life.

Stars

What can you say about them?
They form
higgledy-piggledy patterns
almost a nonsense
which to our eye, always
looking for meaning
translates into a zodiac,
while we take pills
according to the interpretation
of charlatans.

Speckled Universe

I see fragments of a sun
split by infinities
into the normal parameters:
Earth; Moon; stars.
All black, except for
the speckled space
that everything is composed of.

I can't stop there;
inside the wieldy atom
protons, nucleons, quarks
split sub-infinitesimally into
further components. Lurks
behind any of them,
fragmentary meteorites,
the face of the aliens?
Should I smile politely?

The humming world goes by;
inside a test-tube, whole galaxies,
millions of worlds, that it would take
all our evolution to cross to
over a great divide
might be living
breathing
the fire of existence.

What goes on inside
the elements
what goes on outside
this frosty hole?
Look, the world our Earth
is only one of many
green, blue and white-wisped
worlds and
shall we still be alone?

Night

Step out into it
lover of life, go
half-dressed, delirious,
with deep drummings
of insignificance in your life, out
where things are shadows,
and movement is a curse,
because the night
that can be seen
only God knows.

There elements unite
in single triumph
of evolution, dark souls
press their purpose
on every dream.
Heaven is only
the thin moonlit moment
here, that comes between
each tick of nothing,
that presses on nothing,
that is nothing.

Key of Dawn

In the thin hour of night
that comes between first light
and the glory of morning
you will find me.

In the golden tussle of dawn,
where the ancients crashed chariots,
drawing the dead night across
scarlet skies, I may wish to be

hidden. Partly in, mostly out
of this world, its lame ducks
lining up to be crucified:
work; commitment; money.

Let the dogs of dream come after me,
I'll give them a rare chase,
more run for their fun than any fox,
hidden out of time and place.

In a dream, in a night-mare
where the ticking clock fails to come,
where the spirits of children keep alive
the cold hour of calling,

come, be with me, share
with us the secrets long hidden
behind the veil of silent night
unlocked by the key of dawn.

A Puzzle

I did my work
in the Chapel of Remembrance
where people halted
in front of death.

I did my thinking
in the Garden of the Fountain;
there forked paths take you
where you wish to go.

I did my research
in dens of much iniquity
where opinion bubbled
in pipes and minds.

Coursing through the veins
of liberal executives,
the future predicament
showed its signs.

I lived my life,
I brewed it; every day
the cheap liquor of work,
the flashing coins of commerce.

I did my penance
in front of a screen,

its light of indifference
ushered me in.

I did my worship
in halls of lust, where women,
cloaked in mystery, came and went
without acknowledgement.

I left in confusion,
that house of dreams,
showed my devotion
in theatrical scenes.

I walked among heathens,
flirted with whores,
tested the other world
through half-closed doors.

Yet all I could see
was the bluster of science,
the indecision of politics,
the confusion of religion

and many faces laughing,
loving, without knowledge,
praying, without return,
hoping, without belief.

Time

I tell of the lost hours
playing games—in the fun
of distant worlds, and words framed
from disappointment, another hour ticks by.

My disease is tamed, in a circle.
Two remote hands edge, semaphore
to the knowing, ever closer,
now nearer then far apart.

My daughter cannot tell the time,
it doesn't matter to her that things
divide into other things
and then dissolve.

It doesn't matter, to her, that time
is lost, and with it memories,
as if it were not all contained,
as if the brain had failed.

Is it an element then? Time,
or division of the moment, anticipation
over before indulgence,
convenience, or torture?

Dragging us onward, admonishing;
the wagging finger of electronics
or the old Grandfather,
monotonous, severe,

heirloom of the family, that ticks
over arguments
and the door that closes
for the last time.

An Audience

I come from across time.
Centuries old, my family is history.
From past, present and future
the soul is put here
at this infinite now, to learn.

We await our individuation,
our holy turn. Standing there
was the mystery not revealed to me?
I had read, I had learned
not the rote of knowledge,
that school or college,
could offer me
but the bitter breaks and hurts
of relationships, the wounds that love
has inflicted; the truth behind misery.

Forget the reality of senses,
of sight, touch, taste, just go
and stand upon an unknown beach
and listen to me. Be patient,
attend to devotional practise
that the Church doesn't begin to see.
Listen for me.

The Way

One word,
no word,
came the word.
Is this what they meant?
Came the one,
is this what they meant?
Cradled by love
and the complete disaster
of coming.

So, we forced our faith
into a man,
a figure, sacred
flesh but no more
secure.

They followed the Way.
Path, no path
or split, subconscious,
silly era of just belonging?

Not knowing our concerns
that one man could be so kingly,
they followed,
were

absorbed
became
the infinite Tao.
We didn't.

River

Through each of us
a River runs.
No-one knows
from where it comes.
No-one knows
to where it goes:
Only that it flows.

The Path

We travel a road, who knows where it leads?
The darkness leads on, into more darkness.
The plain, unalterable fact of the light
is our only delight.

This path branches, not once, but often,
that we trace our slow steps along;
its route leads only to what is not
from where it was, and while we stop

to consider the various places on
this tortuous road we tread upon,
the misty trees fill the sky
and we die.

In death we awaken, and still move on
for only an image is life, once gone,
where the picture of truth is revealed, to the eye,
but not why.

Fate

Fate, sealed in bones
visits us. Will it be
today or tomorrow? We are gone
leaving only space.

Possessions crumble,
Time holds all,
death of the bones
excepting that the soul

lives in, is evidence:
nothing remains.
Only the life written in books
furnishes an end.

www.ingramcontent.com/pod-product-compliance
Ingram Content Group UK Ltd.
Pitfield, Milton Keynes, MK11 3LW, UK
UKHW041421180426
11947UKWH00007B/233